10B

UFOs: Fact or Fiction?

Nonfiction by

Laura D'Angelo

SCHOLASTIC INC.

New York Toronto London Auckland Sydney
Mexico City New Delhi Hong Kong

Cover photo by

Vladimir Pcholkin/FPG International

Printed in the U.S.A.

ISBN 0-439-05706-X

2 3 4 5 6 7 8 9 10 23 06 05 04 03 02 01 00 99

Table of Contents

The writer, Laura D'Angelo, decides to find out the truth about UFOs.

It was near midnight. I was cruising down the highway. I was singing along with the radio. Suddenly, the music turned to static. I turned the dial. Nothing happened. I heard only a strange hum.

I got a weird feeling. I felt as if I weren't alone. Then I started thinking of stories I'd heard about space aliens.

Were they out tonight? Would a bright light suddenly appear above me? Would it stop the engine of my car? Would tiny aliens drag me into a spaceship?

No! I drove home very fast.

But things at home didn't make me feel much better. Something caught my eye as I opened the door. I looked up. A spaceship was right over my head! It was very still. It looked like it was floating. Then it quickly shot across the sky.

Okay, maybe it wasn't a spaceship. Maybe it was a star or an airplane. At least that's what I told myself.

That night I made a decision. I would find out the truth about space aliens and spaceships. Are they for real?

Do you believe that space aliens are real? Why or why not?

Laura reports on a strange thing that crashed in a desert in New Mexico.

I had always thought that people who saw UFOs (Unidentified Flying Objects) were crazy. After that night, I wasn't so sure. So I started reading about them.

I found a news story from July of 1947. A pilot named Kenneth Arnold had seen weird silver objects in the sky. He said they looked like saucers skipping across water. People started calling them "flying saucers."

Two weeks later, an unidentified flying object crashed in Roswell, New Mexico. Some people said a rancher found parts of it. He supposedly said that the pieces were as thin as tinfoil. But they were also very strong.

The United States government studied them. Then, General Roger Ramey said that they were nothing important. They were just parts of a large weather balloon.

For many people, that was the end of the story. For others, it was just the beginning. They thought that the government was hiding the truth. They believed that an alien spaceship had crashed in Roswell.

They even said that four dead aliens were on board. They claimed to have a movie to prove it. It seemed real. The black-and-white film shows scientists looking at what seems to be very weird alien bodies—and a large black eyeball.

What do you think crashed in the desert at Roswell?

It wasn't a weather balloon at Roswell. Now even the government admits it.

3 Flying Saucers

I kept reading about UFOs. People everywhere said they had seen them.

People in England had seen them.

People in China had seen them.

People in Russia had seen them.

Thousands of people all over the world had reported UFOs.

I started to think that they had to be real.

But maybe they weren't. I kept reading.

I found a new government report about Roswell. It admitted that there really had been a cover-up. A weather balloon had not crashed there.

Neither had a spaceship. According to the government, what really hit the ground was a secret spy tool.

I also found out more about the "alien" movie. It does exist, but it is blurry. It may not show what it claims.

What's more, there's never been any real *proof* of UFOs. No one could show me a crashed spaceship. No one could show me a space alien, dead or alive.

On the other hand, people *could* prove that some of the sightings were fakes.

For example, in 1967, two teenage brothers were throwing a frisbee. They took pictures of it in the air. They told everyone that it was a flying saucer. People believed them for nine years. Then the brothers told the truth. They had made the whole thing up.

Why would someone lie about seeing a flying saucer?

Some people say they have seen aliens up close!

Kidnapped! 4

It seemed to me that UFOs existed only in people's minds. Then I read even more amazing stories. Some people have actually been *abducted* by space aliens! That's what they say, anyway.

In 1961, Betty and Barney Hill were out driving. A flying saucer was following them. Barney pulled over. He looked through his binoculars.

Guess what he saw? Alien eyes were staring back at him through the windows of a UFO !

The Hills blinked. It seemed like a minute went by. It was really two hours.

What could have happened?

The Hills went to see some UFO experts.

These experts hypnotized them. This helped the Hills "remember" that space aliens had "kidnapped" them.

Since then, hundreds of people have told similar stories. They "floated" onto spaceships. There, aliens examined them. Then the aliens put "tracking devices" in their bodies. That way, the aliens could always find the people again.

Afterward, the aliens made these people forget what had happened. Somehow, the aliens blocked the people's memories. But some people remembered anyway. Others remembered when they were hypnotized.

These were interesting stories. I wasn't sure whether or not I believed them.

What do you think happened to Betty and Barney Hill?

Laura talks to some people who say they were kidnapped by space aliens.

I wanted to know more about these abductions. So I called a woman named Beth Collings. She'd written a book about her experiences with aliens. Beth didn't sound at all crazy. Still, her story was really strange.

Beth met a woman named Anna in 1987. They'd never seen each other before. But they felt like they'd always been friends.

Two years later, Beth had some scary dreams about her childhood. In these dreams, she was in some kind of strange laboratory. There, she made friends with a little girl in a school uniform.

Beth began drawing pictures of these dreams. One day, Anna saw one of Beth's drawings. It was a picture of a large, four-

fingered hand. It was the hand of an alien.

Anna was really scared by it. Then Beth started telling Anna about her memories of the lab. Anna started filling in the blanks. She already knew the story that Beth was telling!

That's when they came to a conclusion. They had actually met 30 years before! As children, they had played together on an alien spaceship. Anna had been the girl in the school uniform!

"The aliens put us in a room with other kids," Beth said. "They were odd children, like dolls. They didn't respond."

Beth and Anna say abduction experiences run in their families. Space creatures had also studied their relatives. Beth's 74-year-old father showed her pictures he had drawn as a child. One was a scary four-fingered hand.

> Do you think aliens kidnapped Beth and Anna?

Many people honestly believe that aliens kidnapped them. Does that mean it's true?

Alien Beliefs 6

My next stop was the public library. There, I found shelves filled with UFO books. One was called *Abduction: Human Encounters with Aliens*. A professor named John Mack had written it.

Mack believes that aliens communicate with humans all the time. They do it by using thought waves.

People who are kidnapped by aliens often feel as if the aliens know what they're thinking, Mack said. They may even feel that aliens have taken over their minds.

That's pretty scary.

I wanted to know more. So I called John Carpenter. He's a social worker who's done a lot of research on abductions.

Carpenter has hypnotized more than a hundred "abductees." Their strong feelings about their experiences make him think that their stories are true.

"These people are right there in front of you," he said. "They burst into tears talking about those big black eyes. It gives you a chill you'll never forget."

Talking to Carpenter gave me the creeps! He sounded smart. He also sounded like he was telling the truth. He really believes that aliens are stealing people from their homes.

I began to think that the stories might be true after all.

If space aliens had come to America, what kind of proof might there be?

UFOs in the Movies

For almost as long as there have been movies, there have been aliens in the movies.

Lots of movies have answered these questions: What would aliens look like? How would they travel? And what if they came to earth?!

Here's a poster from a 1951 movie, *The Man From Planet X.* These aliens didn't look much different from you or me!

AMERICAN INTERNATIONAL PICTURES

Yikes! Here's what the aliens looked like in the 1957 movie, *Invasion of the Saucermen.*

A scientist takes a look at an alien in *The X-Files Movie,* made in 1998. It doesn't take an expert to tell that these aliens were pretty creepy.

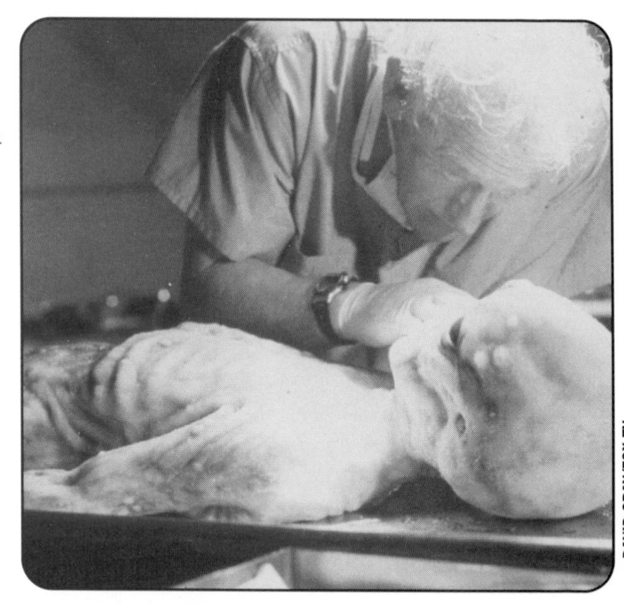

DAVID GRAY/FOX TV

It's a bird! It's a plane! No, it's an alien spaceship! This shot is from *Close Encounters of the Third Kind,* a movie made in 1977.

20TH CENTURY FOX

Twenty years later, Unidentified Flying Objects (UFOs) looked a lot cooler. This is the spaceship from the 1996 movie, *Independence Day*.

In most movies, a visit from aliens was bad news. In the film *Earth Versus Flying Saucers,* aliens attack the U.S. government in Washington, D.C.

The 1997 movie, *Contact,* was unusual. Jodie Foster plays a scientist who argues that aliens mean no harm. They just want to communicate.

With friends like these, who needs enemies? In *Strange Invaders,* aliens arrive in a small town. They hypnotize everyone and take over. This movie was made in 1983.

REAL UFOs?!

Now, back to the real world. . . . Many people say that they have seen UFOs and have taken pictures of them. Here are some of the most famous photos. Some are fakes. Some are mistakes.

AND THE OTHERS . . . ?

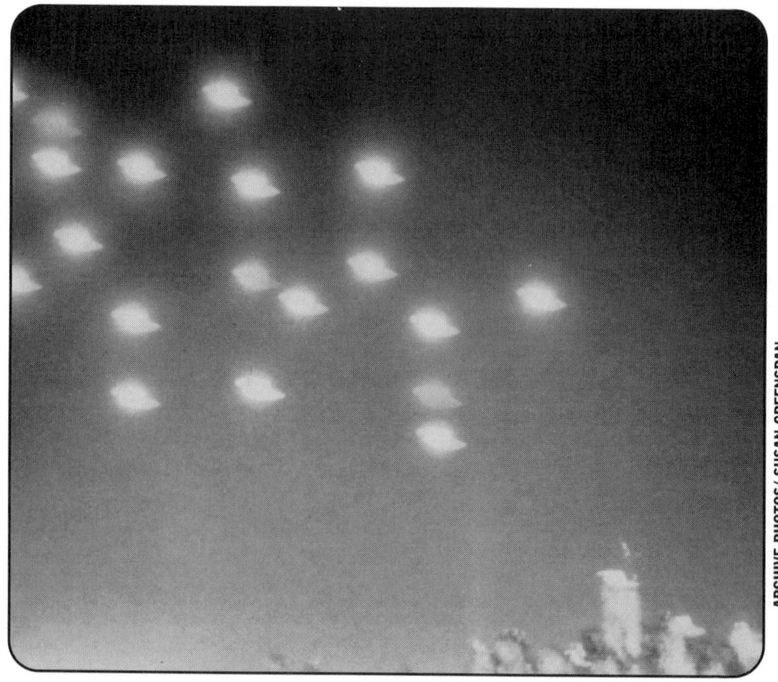

ARCHIVE PHOTOS/ SUSAN GREENSPAN

In this 1989 photo, UFOs seem to float over New York City. (The city is on the bottom right.) Sorry, this picture turned out to be a big fake.

ARCHIVE PHOTOS

See those four blobs? Some say they are UFOs, flying over Salem, Massachusetts, in 1952.

REUTERS/HANDOUT–U.S. AIRFORCE/ARCHIVE PHOTOS

In 1972, people in New Mexico saw this object and thought it was a UFO. It turned out that it was really part of the space program.

So what do you think? Do aliens and UFOs only exist in the movies? Or could there really be something out there? If you're not sure, keep your eyes on the sky and your camera by your side!

Space aliens are supposed to be smart. But they sure don't they act like it.

I needed to get back down to earth. I decided to talk to someone who thinks UFOs aren't real. Philip Klass has spent 30 years proving that stories about aliens aren't true.

I said I thought some stories *could* be true.

"Oh, come on," he said. "Imagine if aliens were breaking into our homes. Let's say there was some proof. What do you think our government would do? It would be politicians' number-one issue!"

He did have a point.

Klass had some other good points. Aliens are supposed to come from advanced worlds, right? So why don't they ever give humans useful information?

"If they say anything, it's always

something really obvious," Klass says. "They say 'don't pollute' or 'don't fight nuclear wars.' They never say, 'You have a problem with cancer. We had that same problem on our planet. Let us tell you how to cure it. . . .'"

Klass also thinks that higher life forms would have more sense. Why would they travel such long distances to abduct people again and again? They could just bring some people back with them.

> If you were an alien, would you come to Earth? What would you try to do here?

For many people, UFOs are a real-life nightmare. . . .

Are They Dreaming? 8

Philip Klass raised some good questions. Still, I had some of my own. Why would thousands of people make up these tales? And why would their stories be so similar?

Klass told me that psychologists have thought about these questions. He suggested that I talk to one of them. So I did.

I called Steven Lynn, a professor in New York. He said that UFO experts who treat abductees may actually be helping to "create" their stories.

How? Under hypnosis, people are often very open to suggestions, Lynn told me. They may start to imagine the things that the hypnotist is asking them about.

That made sense. Still, I wondered why the

stories were all so similar.

It's easy to fake abduction stories, Lynn said. Everyone knows the basic tale.

To prove it, Lynn did an experiment. He asked college students to make up their own abduction stories. Their stories were just like the ones that the "abductees" tell.

There's a simple reason for this, he says. Abduction tales are on TV and in the movies. Everyone has seen and heard them. No wonder these stories all sound alike.

"Let's say that I go into a kindergarten class and ask the kids to draw pictures of Santa Claus. Their pictures all look similar. Does that mean Santa exists?" Lynn asked.

Did you ever wake up from a dream and feel as though it had actually happened?

Laura concludes that there aren't UFOs out there. Or at least she thinks there aren't!

THE TRUTH 9

I hung up the phone. I'd come to the end of my study. I'd explored both sides. I was pretty sure that we're alone on Earth. At least, I think we're alone, so far.

So what was that weird thing above my house? It could have been anything, right?

Okay, I guess there's a part of me that thinks there *could* be something out there.

I'll leave it to you to take over this case. Maybe someday you'll prove that UFOs exist. Or maybe you'll prove that every story is a trick. When you find out, let me know!

What steps could you take to find out if space aliens are real?

Did you like this book?

Here are two other READ 180 Paperbacks that you might like to read.

Crazy For Chocolate

Travel back in time to find out about the delicious history of chocolate.

By Frieda Wishinsky

Odd Jobs

True stories about people who wrestle alligators, clean skyscrapers, guide airplanes, and perform in Broadway theaters—all to earn a living!

By John DiConsiglio

GLOSSARY

abducted kidnapped

abductees people who have been abducted

abduction a kidnapping

advanced ahead of everyone or everything else

aliens creatures from other planets

binoculars an instrument that you look through to see things in the distance

conclusion arriving at a decision or understanding

cover-up a plan to hide the truth

hypnotized putting someone into a trance

lab short for *laboratory*

laboratory a room or building containing special equipment for people to use in scientific experiments

politicians people who run for and hold government offices

pollute to litter; to make dirty or impure

professor a teacher at a college

psychologist	someone who studies people's minds and emotions, and the way that they behave
similar	alike, or of the same type
static	crackling noises on the radio or television